Polio Epidemic

Other titles in the *American Disasters* series:

The Challenger Disaster
Tragic Space Flight
ISBN 0-7660-1222-0

Mount St. Helens Volcano
Violent Eruption
ISBN 0-7660-1552-1

The Exxon Valdez
Tragic Oil Spill
ISBN 0-7660-1058-9

The Oklahoma City Bombing
Terror in the Heartland
ISBN 0-7660-1061-9

Fire in Oakland, California
Billion-Dollar Blaze
ISBN 0-7660-1220-4

Plains Outbreak Tornadoes
Killer Twisters
ISBN 0-7660-1059-7

Hurricane Andrew
Nature's Rage
ISBN 0-7660-1057-0

San Francisco Earthquake, 1989
Death and Destruction
ISBN 0-7660-1060-0

The L.A. Riots
Rage in the City of Angels
ISBN 0-7660-1219-0

The Siege at Waco
Deadly Inferno
ISBN 0-7660-1218-2

Love Canal
Toxic Waste Tragedy
ISBN 0-7660-1553-X

TWA Flight 800
Explosion in Midair
ISBN 0-7660-1217-4

The Mighty Midwest Flood
Raging Rivers
ISBN 0-7660-1221-2

The World Trade Center Bombing
Terror in the Towers
ISBN 0-7660-1056-2

Polio Epidemic

Crippling Virus Outbreak

Victoria Sherrow

AMERICAN
DISASTERS

Enslow Publishers, Inc.

40 Industrial Road   PO Box 38
Box 398   Aldershot
Berkeley Heights, NJ 07922   Hants GU12 6BP
USA   UK

http://www.enslow.com

Library of Congress Cataloging-in-Publication Data

Sherrow, Victoria.
    Polio epidemic : crippling virus outbreak / by Victoria Sherrow.
       p. cm. — (American disasters)
    Includes bibliographical references and index.
    ISBN 0-7660-1555-6
    1. Poliomyelitis—United States—History—20th century—Juvenile
literature. [1. Poliomyelitis—History. 2. Diseases—History. 3.
Epidemics—History.]
    I. Title. II. Series.
    RA644.P9 S44 2001
    614.5'49'09730904—dc21
                            00-009472

Printed in the United States of America

10 9 8 7 6 5 4 3 2 1

To Our Readers:
We have done our best to make sure all Internet addresses in this book were
active and appropriate when we went to press. However, the author and the
publisher have no control over and assume no liability for the material
available on those Internet sites or on other Web sites they may link to. Any
comments or suggestions can be sent by e-mail to comments@enslow.com or
to the address on the back cover.

Illustration Credits: AP/Wide World Photos, pp. 1, 9, 24, 25, 33, 38, 39; The
March of Dimes, pp. 6, 12, 14, 15, 16, 19, 22, 28, 30, 34, 35, 37.

Cover Illustration: The March of Dimes.

Contents

FIGHT POLIO!

prevention

treatment

Join the **MARCH OF DIMES**

The National Foundation for Infantile Para...

Outbreaks of polio in the United States and Canada were common in the early 1950s. Posters like the one above encouraged contributions to the March of Dimes to help fight the disease.

CHAPTER 1

Summer Fears

Americans had many reasons to feel hopeful in 1952. World War II had been over for seven years. The economy was strong and home sales reached new highs. Science and technology were changing people's lives. Washing machines, vacuum cleaners, dishwashers, and other appliances made housework easier.

Many families had just bought their first television sets. People enjoyed "I Love Lucy," "Dragnet," and other popular shows. Sports also drew big audiences. In baseball, the New York Yankees were expected to win the World Series. Summer brought good times at pools, parks, campsites, and beaches.

But summer also brought fear of a terrible disease called polio. Polio is a disease that can paralyze its victims. It usually begins with a headache, fever, or sore throat. Then the muscles might become stiff or weak. Some people recover after just a few days. Others might spend weeks or many months in the hospital. Polio leaves some victims physically disabled. Most victims are children, but adults can also get polio.

By 1952, outbreaks of polio had swept across the United States and Canada every year since 1916. It sometimes hit hundreds, even thousands, of people in one city. These outbreaks occurred most often in warm weather.

"People feared summer," recalled Dr. William Foege, a professor in Atlanta. "They actually closed the swimming pools, and then closed the theatres. And then even churches would stop having services because people did not want to get together."[1]

Dr. Ralph Chase had cared for many polio victims in San Angelo, Texas. "We got to the point where few people trusted one another," he said. "Few of them would shake hands."[2]

Many polio patients could not move their arms. Others could not walk. Some victims could not speak or even breathe. The disease could kill people if they were unable to breathe. Those who could not breathe on their own had to be placed inside big, metal tanks called iron lungs.

An iron lung is a very large respirator. Respirators are machines that help people breathe. Iron lungs covered the whole body except the head. Air pressure inside the tanks went up and down. This forced air in and out of the patient's lungs. One nurse described the iron lung as a "huge rigid coffin standing on four legs and attached to a large electric pump."[3]

People were terrified at the thought of having to live out their lives inside an iron lung. In an effort to fight

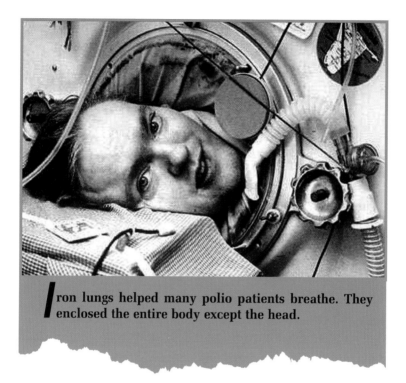

*I*ron lungs helped many polio patients breathe. They enclosed the entire body except the head.

polio, many Americans donated dimes to a charity called the March of Dimes. This charity helped care for polio patients and fund research for a cure for this awful disease. People could only hope that a cure might someday be found. Until then, there was nothing anyone could do to guard against polio. It could strike anyone at any time.

Nineteen-year-old Hugh Gallagher was a college student in Philadelphia in 1952. That summer, he was invited to join other students traveling by dogsled to the North Pole. But the sweeping polio epidemic would keep him from ever making the trip.

For Gallagher, polio began with a cold that would not go away. After ten days, he felt very sick. He later said,

"My neck was very stiff, my spine was aching, I had terrible pain."[4] It hurt to walk but it hurt to lie down, too. A few days later, he felt even worse. A doctor at the college health center gave him a pill for the pain and he went to sleep. Gallagher recalled waking up the next morning:

> It was a beautiful sunny day, about six in the morning. The sun was streaming in the room and I lay there and watched as my legs became paralyzed. First the left leg moving up, and then the right leg moving down.[5]

Gallagher was taken to a Philadelphia hospital. By then he was totally paralyzed and needed an iron lung. He would use it for the next eight weeks until he could breathe on his own again.

Terror spread during 1952 as approximately 58,000 people were stricken with polio. More than 3,000 of them died. People heard the names of the latest victims on local radio stations. Newspapers also kept track of them. Some papers printed maps showing the streets where people with polio lived. White circles meant that someone living there had been paralyzed. Black circles meant someone had died.

Millions of Americans feared they might be next.

CHAPTER 2

A Crippling Virus

The number of polio cases around the world rose sharply after 1900. Yet the disease itself dates back thousands of years.

Skeletons with signs of polio have been found in ancient tombs. Old Egyptian carvings show people with shrunken legs and arms that look like the result of polio. Ancient Greek doctors described a paralyzing illness that might also have been polio.

Doctors in Europe wrote about it in the 1700s. Scientists wondered what caused it. Was it a disease of the stomach? A strange fever? Something in the air? Nobody knew.

An Italian doctor, Giovanni Monteggia, treated children with the disease in the early 1800s. Their sickness began with a fever. Later, the children's arms and legs hung limp and motionless. The doctor wrote, "No movement is made when the sole of the foot is tickled."[1]

*T*his ancient Egyptian slab shows a man with a shrunken leg leaning on a staff. It may be the earliest known evidence of polio.

Around this same time, Dr. Jakob Von Heine was treating victims in Germany. He noticed that they did not develop brain damage. Therefore, Von Heine said, the disease must attack motor nerves in the spinal cord. These nerves control muscle movements.

The first known epidemics of the disease occurred in the 1800s. An epidemic is when a disease spreads to many people over a large area very quickly. In 1887, 44 cases were reported in Sweden. Another outbreak affected 132 people in Vermont in 1894. It was about this time that doctors began calling the disease poliomyelitis— polio for short.

A Swedish doctor named Karl Oscar Medin made a big discovery during an epidemic in 1905. He realized that the disease was being passed from person to person. In other words, polio was contagious. But nobody knew what caused it. Doctors could not prevent or cure polio and there was no effective treatment.

In 1908, Karl Landsteiner, an American scientist who was born in Austria, discovered the virus that causes polio. A virus is a microscopic organism that lives inside the cells of other living things and causes disease. Discovering the virus meant that there might be a way to prevent polio.

Scientists talked about making a vaccine. Vaccines are treatments that help make people immune to a disease. People who are immune to a disease will not get sick from it. Vaccines usually contain a weakened or dead virus. This produces antibodies without actually causing the disease. Antibodies are proteins that help protect the body from foreign substances.

In 1916, a terrible polio epidemic hit New York City. More than 27,000 people became paralyzed. More than 7,000 died. City residents tried to stop polio from spreading. City workers covered all the trash cans to prevent spreading germs. The streets of New York were flooded with water in an effort to keep them clean. Many public places were closed. People tied pieces of cloth soaked in camphor around their necks. This strong-smelling chemical was thought to keep germs away.

People were afraid and upset. Some blamed polio on the many poor immigrants who lived in New York. They said polio spread among people who did not keep their bodies and homes clean. But later epidemics showed that polio could strike anyone. It hit the rich as well as the poor. It affected people of all colors. It struck in all regions, on farms as well as in cities.

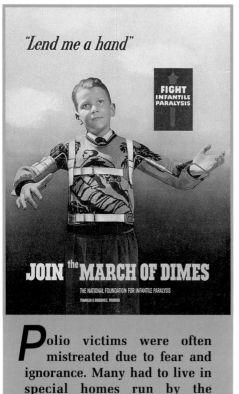

"Lend me a hand"

FIGHT INFANTILE PARALYSIS

JOIN the MARCH OF DIMES

THE NATIONAL FOUNDATION FOR INFANTILE PARALYSIS

FRANKLIN D. ROOSEVELT, FOUNDER

*P*olio victims were often mistreated due to fear and ignorance. Many had to live in special homes run by the government.

Polio victims suffered from much prejudice as well. Some people avoided them or looked away when they saw a person who was stricken. Children with polio might be sent to separate schools out of fear of spreading the disease. Many lived in special homes run by the government. Such places often had grim names. One was called "Home for the Incurables." Another was the "Home for the Destitute Crippled Children."

As the 1930s arrived, no cure was in sight. Epidemics continued to strike the United States in 1936, 1937, 1941, 1944, 1946, 1949, and 1951. Some places were hit hard. Detroit had an average of 2,500 cases of polio each year during the 1940s. In 1943, one in every 200 children in Fort Worth, Texas, got polio. Two Fort Worth hospitals struggled to help 186 victims. A local newspaper reported that "iron lungs and patients' beds overflowed into the halls."[2]

Some cities built hospitals just for polio patients. Others turned older hospitals into polio treatment centers. One was Children's Hospital in Akron, Ohio. It served children from the Ohio area during various epidemics. In 1944, the hospital had 208 polio patients. More than 1,000 people in Ohio got polio that year.

People across the country lived in fear. Jo Walker was one of many victims in Philadelphia. She was stricken in August, 1944. In the hospital, the six-year-old Walker lay inside a glass cubicle. She heard another girl screaming as doctors performed a test. Then a minister came. Walker recalled thinking, "Why would he be there unless I was going to die?"[3]

Polio researchers worked hard to make a vaccine. But as 1952 arrived, no vaccine was ready. Americans were about to face the worst polio epidemic in history.

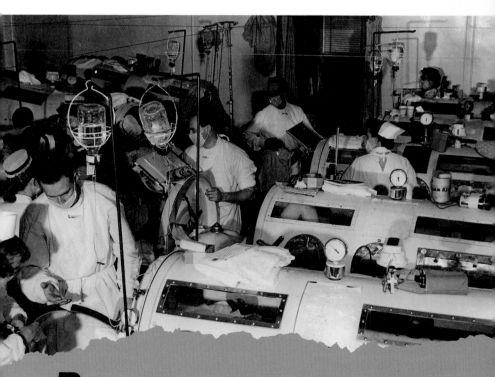

*P*olio epidemics continued to strike the United States throughout the 1930s and 1940s. In some hospitals, iron lungs overflowed into hallways.

"Look! I can walk again

Throughout the polio epidemic of 1952, many young polio patients struggled to recover from the paralyzing effects of the disease.

CHAPTER 3

Quarantine!

All summer in 1952, parents throughout America watched their children carefully because of the polio epidemic. They rushed to the hospital or called a doctor if their child had a fever, headache, or runny nose. In those days, doctors often made house calls. Dr. Hugh McAdams practiced medicine in Lafayette, Indiana. He remembered, "If a mother called and said her child had a fever and a headache, you had to go see, because it might be polio."[1]

Young polio patients fought for their lives. They needed help to eat or drink. Swallowing was a chore. They could not wipe their foreheads when they were hot. They could not swat a mosquito or fly that landed on their body. When they cried, they could not wipe their own tears.

Adults were also stricken with polio. In 1952, there were more adult cases than in any previous polio epidemic. Many of them were doctors and nurses.

Ambulance bells clanged as patients were rushed to hospitals. A nurse who worked in Pittsburgh, Pennsylvania, recalled that time. "There were sixteen or seventeen new admissions every day," she said. "You'd hear a child crying for someone to read his mail to him or for a drink of water or [to explain] why she can't move. . . . It was an atmosphere of grief, terror, and helpless rage. It was horrible."[2]

Polio cases arose from coast to coast. There were 1,203 polio victims in Chicago alone. Hundreds were left paralyzed, and 82 people died there. Other large cities reported more than a thousand cases. A former Dallas resident said, "In the news every day was a tally of the polio cases—like today they total up the car crashes on holiday weekends. Every day they would report 'another so many polio cases today.'"[3]

People dreaded seeing signs that read "Quarantine!" or "Polio—Keep Out." These warnings appeared on the door of the house when somebody had polio. Nobody could visit for at least several days. People in the house could not have contact with others.

Door-to-door salesmen sold polio insurance in some cities. People put poison inside their garbage cans. They feared that flies and mosquitoes carried polio germs and hoped the poison would kill these pests. City councils shut down theaters, churches, and schools. Camps and Sunday schools were closed. Children saw empty seats in their schoolrooms. Often, this meant another classmate had polio.

Playgrounds stood empty, too. Fearful parents kept their children at home. They hoped to avoid other people's germs. Some children complained about missing their favorite activities. Parents were heard to say, "Do you want to end up in an iron lung?"[4]

Hospitals separated polio patients from others. They

*C*hildren were often afraid of iron lungs. But for many of them, it was the only way they were able to breathe. Many more needed leg braces to walk or stand upright.

were often kept in glass cubicles. This was done to prevent polio from spreading. Another reason was to keep polio patients safe from other infections. Doctors and nurses wore gowns, gloves, and masks around these patients.

Doctors said the polio virus stayed alive on a patient's belongings. Schools had to burn a sick child's desk and everything in his or her locker. Amy Gardner's daughter Glynda was only eighteen months old when she was struck with polio in 1952. She recalled what her husband Ed went through after the doctor told them to burn all of their daughter's belongings:

> He piled all her things in plastic bags and carried them out to the alley where we had a burning barrel. He burned her frilly little dresses that I had made for her and every stitch of clothing she had, along with all her bed-sheets and baby blankets. He burned her little shoes and then the hardest part of all was when he began to burn her toys. He cried as he tossed them into the barrel, one at a time, saving her beloved favorite doll for last. He knew how she loved it and it hurt to toss it into the burning barrel. . . . He cried his heart out.[5]

Sick children often could not see their parents for weeks or months. Hospitals did not allow many visitors. Sometimes, parents could only visit their sick children on Sunday afternoons. Many polio hospitals were far away from people's hometowns. Families traveled hours to visit their loved ones and could not get there often. Carol Boyer was three years old and living near Washington, D.C., when she became ill in 1952. She later recalled:

They put you in a white hospital bed with the bars up. . . . At three years old they were afraid you were going to fall out. . . . I remember it was awful being left alone without my mom. I just cried and cried and cried.[6]

Like many children, Boyer thought the iron lungs looked frightening. "That was very scary to me," she said, "to see people that had to be flat on their backs, only their heads stuck out of this big, white, cylindrical machine. I thought they didn't have bodies. I was afraid of what was happening to these people."[7]

Storms and other problems could also cause life-and-death emergencies. When the electricity went off, nurses had to pump the iron lungs by hand. Robina Parker was a nurse during those years. She said, "The iron lungs were frightening contraptions and the patients were terrified of them."[8]

Iron lungs might look scary, but they saved lives. Omega Baker recalled how it felt to be inside the iron lung at age five. "The only sounds I hear are the hum of the motor, the click, and 'whoosh' as the air is pushed in and out."[9] Nurses fed her through a tube because she could not use her mouth and throat muscles to chew and swallow. Liquids went through this tube and into her stomach.

Four-year-old Diane Kirlin spent 159 days in a hospital in Philadelphia in the summer of 1952. She later said that she could not see the row of iron lungs from her bed. But she could hear the noise they made. She recalled, "When the nurses would turn one off, you knew that a child had died. Then they would roll the iron lung away."[10]

Nobody knew how long they would need an iron lung. It might be days, weeks, or months. A few people would need help to breathe for the rest of their lives.

A research team working at the University of Pittsburgh was working hard to find a cure for polio. Led by Dr. Jonas Salk, they developed a potential vaccine for polio in 1952. But it could not be used right away. First the vaccine had to be carefully tested for a couple of years to prove that it was safe and effective.

In the meantime, thousands of people were fighting polio. They and their loved ones faced many problems.

*D*r. Jonas Salk (right) and Dr. P. L. Bazely are shown hard at work in the laboratory.

CHAPTER 4

A Brave Fight

As the number of polio cases mounted, hospitals needed more supplies. They had to hire more nurses and extra people. These things cost money. Help came from the March of Dimes.

The March of Dimes was started in 1938 because of a famous man who had polio. President Franklin D. Roosevelt had caught the disease in 1921 at age thirty-nine. His legs were left paralyzed. He found a place to exercise in Warm Springs, Georgia. The water there was said to aid healing. Swimming in the warm pool made Roosevelt feel stronger, although his legs were still paralyzed. He turned Warm Springs into a polio treatment center. Other people came to use the pool and do special exercises. They also learned skills for everyday living.

Roosevelt served as president of the United States for more than twelve years, starting in 1933. In 1938, he asked his friend Basil O'Connor to head an organization to help polio victims. The organization would raise

*F*ranklin Delano Roosevelt caught polio in 1921 and was confined to a wheelchair as a result. Eleven years later, he was elected president.

money for research and treatment. It was called the National Foundation for Infantile Paralysis. (Polio was also called "infantile paralysis" because it usually struck young children.) The foundation was later renamed the March of Dimes.

The March of Dimes led one of the biggest fundraising efforts in history. The money they raised helped thousands of polio patients. It paid for their braces, crutches, and other equipment. It also paid for the services they needed. Some of the money was used to train professionals who helped people recover from polio.

In 1946, the March of Dimes chose its first "poster child." He was Donald Anderson. Each year, a new child appeared on posters designed to show people the need for donations. The children wore braces and used crutches. Some sat in wheelchairs. These brave children gave a "face" to polio statistics.

Americans knew the March of Dimes was funding polio vaccine research. They saw the organization helping people in their communities, too. During the 1952 epidemic, the demand for iron lungs was so great that hospitals ran short. The March of Dimes bought more iron lungs for them.

As a doctor in Cleveland, Ohio, recalled, "We ran out of respirators. The March of Dimes had to find some. . . . It was a horrible business. My own daughter got polio."[1]

The March of Dimes raised $40 million in 1952. But it could barely pay the costs for such a large epidemic. Some polio patients needed help for months or years. Some needed help for their whole lives. The road back to health was often difficult.

Leaving the iron lung was a big step for many people. Hugh Gallagher recalled his struggle to breathe without it.

*P*resident Roosevelt (left) is shown swimming at the polio treatment center in Warm Springs, Georgia, in 1935.

He said that his therapist "began minute by minute and then [doubled] the time each day until the point where I could breathe on my own for two hours. Then I'd be taken out of the lung and put on a bed."[2]

Lawrence Becker of Nebraska spent nearly a year in an iron lung in 1952. The first time he tried to breathe without it was frightening. He said, "It was like somebody pushed my head under water."[3] The thirteen-year-old Becker kept trying.

"The weaning process was quite brutal," he recalled. "It was with a stopwatch. . . . They would give little prizes for each advance: 'Three minutes . . . all right, you can have a football.' By that time, I didn't want a football. I wanted a chess set."[4]

Each day brought more tests and treatments. But none of it did much good. One doctor recalled, "[Before] the polio vaccine, there wasn't much we could do. We'd put hot packs on their legs to reduce the tension in the muscles, but that didn't stop the polio. . . . They either got better, got worse or died."[5]

Methods of treating polio had changed after the 1930s. Doctors used to put plaster casts on patients' arms and legs. They tried to keep these limbs motionless, often for several months or more. Doctors feared that healthy muscles would pull on the weak ones and damage them.

By 1952, most polio patients were receiving the Kenny treatment instead. Elizabeth Kenny (1880–1952) was an Australian nurse who disagreed with the old treatment methods. She saw that people remained crippled and was deeply upset by their suffering. She said, "My heart was torn with sorrow."[6]

Kenny knew that spasms made muscles tight and shorter. A spasm is when a muscle twitches involuntarily. She put very hot, wet packs of wool on the muscles to relax the spasms. This treatment could go on for an hour. Exercises came next. Kenny pointed out that muscles weaken if they are not used. Movement brings blood into the muscle tissues. Nutrients in the blood help muscles to heal. Kenny's patients were able to move their muscles. The muscles were stretched out slowly to their normal length.

Doctors did not accept Kenny's methods at first. In 1940, she left Australia for the United States. There, she founded a treatment center in Minneapolis and showed people her methods. By the 1950s, the Kenny treatment was widely used.

The hot packs could feel uncomfortable. The exercises hurt. Some people cried during the treatments. But as one man later said, "We had to admit we felt better after their torture."[7]

Patients struggled with pain and disappointment. Edward M. Egan, who later became the Catholic archbishop of Chicago, recalled his struggle with polio at ten years old. "I must confess that I often cried," he said. "After three full months, I still could not be pulled into a sitting position."[8]

Moving a hand or finger, or just wiggling one's toes, was progress. Each step forward was a cause to celebrate.

People rejoiced when they could feed themselves or use a wheelchair. They cheered when they could turn the pages of a book.

Polio survivors felt nervous when they tried to stand up again. They feared their legs would collapse. For many, the next step was being fitted with metal braces. Braces wrapped around the back, legs, or arms to support the weakened muscles. Those who were learning to walk

*P*resident Roosevelt (left) and Basil O'Connor count dimes for the March of Dimes.

again used walking sticks or crutches. Others stayed in wheelchairs. About 1 percent could not leave their beds.

Hugh Gallagher spent two years in a Philadelphia hospital. Then he went to Warm Springs to recover further. He described the skills he and others worked on:

> Learning how to transfer from your bed to a wheelchair, from a wheelchair to a car. How to stand up, if you had the strength to do that. And we learned by watching others. Old [patients] would come back for checkups and there were a lot of [polio patients] who lived on the campus.[9]

People faced more challenges after they returned home. They had to continue their exercises. Often, their parents took charge of the treatment. One or more times a day, their muscles were massaged, stretched, and moved around.

Margaret Stewart of Atlanta, Georgia, learned to walk short distances with a brace and crutches. Using her wheelchair was easier for shopping or going to church. Stewart needed surgery to help straighten her feet at age six and again at age twelve.

Stewart says she was lucky at school. Classmates helped her carry her books. They would change the rules of their games so she could play along with them. She said her family and her religious faith gave her strength.[10]

Other polio survivors recalled problems at school. Sharon Karber said, "Grade school years were very difficult because of my braces and crutches. It was impossible to run and play like other kids. I required leg surgeries . . . every summer until I was 12 years old."[11]

Your dimes did this for me!

FIGHT INFANTILE PARALYSIS

JOIN the MARCH of DIMES
JANUARY 14-31

THE NATIONAL FOUNDATION FOR INFANTILE PARALYSIS, INC

FRANKLIN D. ROOSEVELT, FOUNDER

Donald Anderson, shown in this poster, became the March of Dimes' first poster child in 1946.

Other kinds of problems arose. Many polio victims needed special shoes. Often, one foot was one or two sizes smaller than the other. One leg might also be shorter. A woman in Ohio said her brother hated to go shopping. He was embarrassed when people saw his feet. His mother drew outlines of his feet on pieces of paper. She took them to the store and bought shoes for him.

Sandi Hall recalled her teenage years. She said, "I remember the painful surgeries and the daily exercises. I remember being a kid that was lonely and alone but all the while just wanting to be like all the other kids. . . . I had to go to a special school, see a special doctor, wear special shoes, a back brace and special clothes."[12]

The March of Dimes brought these survivors together. They had chapters in towns all over America. They planned special activities for children who had had polio. For example, they took them on free trips to the circus, the zoo, the movies, and other places. The March of Dimes ran day camps, too.

As 1952 ended, Americans realized just how many people had been stricken. About 58,000 people of different ages had caught polio. More than 3,000 had died. More than 20,000 had been paralyzed. How many more people would suffer from this disease?

CHAPTER 5

"Freedom from Fear"

By 1952, work on the polio vaccine was going well. Dr. Jonas Salk led the research team working at the University of Pittsburgh. Salk was a native of New York City and a medical doctor. His specialty was vaccine research. He was determined to win the battle against polio. The March of Dimes provided much of the money for this research.

Scientists had identified three major types of polio virus. Salk's team knew their vaccine must work against all three types. The vaccine would be made from killed polio viruses. Killed rabies viruses had been used to make a vaccine against rabies. Salk said these dead polio viruses would not cause a person to get polio. But they would still cause the body to make antibodies to the polio virus. Those antibodies would protect people against future attacks of polio.

The research team in Pittsburgh saw the effects of the 1952 epidemic. They felt the urgent need to finish their work. Research assistant Elsie Ward recalled, "Dr. Salk was in the lab morning, afternoon, and night. He couldn't wait to see what was going to happen."[1]

Dr. Julius Youngner was another key part of the team. He recalled, "You can't imagine the excitement of seeing this come to pass under your very fingers."[2]

The vaccine was first tested during 1952. Jonas Salk thought the vaccine was safe. He tested it on himself. Members of the research team also agreed to take the vaccine. Salk later said, "You wouldn't do unto others that

*D*r. Jonas Salk is honored outside the White House on April 22, 1955. Salk received a citation from President Eisenhower and a congressional gold medal for "great achievement in the field of medicine."

*Y*oung "Polio Pioneers" are shown here after receiving their polio vaccinations in 1954.

which you wouldn't do unto yourself."[3] Salk's wife and sons also took the vaccine. It was in the form of an injection, or "shot."

The vaccine could not be given to millions of people yet. A large scientific test was needed. In 1954, Americans were glad to hear that the vaccine trials would soon begin.

Nearly 2 million children throughout the United States took part in the vaccine trials. They were called "Polio Pioneers" and were students in first, second, and third grade. Jane S. Smith was one of them. She was a first-grader in New York City at the time. Her parents signed a form to let her to take part. The epidemic of 1952 had scared parents all over America. Smith wrote, "It's no surprise that my parents, like millions of others, gratefully volunteered their child."[4]

That spring and summer, the children were given shots of a pink-colored liquid. Some children received the vaccine. Others received a placebo, which looked the same but did not contain any vaccine. Another million children did not receive any shot at all. Scientists would compare the children in all three groups.

For nearly a year, scientists gathered information. People around the world waited eagerly to hear the results of the vaccine trials. Scientists announced the outcome in

Elvis Presley receives a shot of Salk's polio vaccine from Dr. Harold Fuerst and Dr. Leona Baumgartner in 1956.

April, 1955. Dr. Thomas Francis headed the team that had judged the test results. He told the waiting crowd, "The new Salk vaccine works, is safe, effective and potent."[5]

Television and radio stations broadcast the news. Across America, people celebrated. Church bells rang. A man in New Jersey painted "Thank you, Dr. Salk" on his store window. Jonas Salk was hailed as a hero. People were urged to get vaccinated, and millions did.

In 1957, Dr. Albert Sabin brought out a different kind of vaccine. Sabin was an American scientist who was born in Poland. He had been working at the University of Cincinnati. His vaccine used weakened live viruses instead of killed viruses. People could take it orally (by mouth). A few drops of vaccine were placed on a sugar cube, then the cube was eaten. For several years, Salk's vaccine was more popular in America than Sabin's. However, by the 1960s, the Sabin vaccine was more widely used.

Most Americans were just thankful these vaccines existed. They did not have to fear polio epidemics anymore. Dr. Malcolm C. Lancaster said, "Seeing polio go away was like witnessing a major miracle."[6] Basil O'Connor, the man who had founded the organization that paid for the research, said the vaccine was "a planned miracle."[7]

By 1995, forty years had passed since the announcement that Salk's vaccine worked. Dr. Jonas Salk remembered his thoughts at that time. He told reporters that the most important result of the vaccine was "freedom from fear."[8]

By 2000, only a few cases of polio occurred in the United States each year. But polio was still a health threat elsewhere. About 35,000 to 40,000 cases are reported each year around the world. The disease is a problem in 116 countries. It occurs mostly in places with poor waste disposal and unclean water.

Some young people in America have never heard of polio. But millions of other people remember it well. Some of them survived polio.

Sadly, the disease goes on

A merchant in Hohokus, New Jersey, expresses his gratitude to Dr. Salk with a sign in his store window.

for some survivors. Many only began having muscle pain and weakness decades after they caught polio. Doctors call this relapse "post-polio syndrome." They think it happens because certain muscles are overworked. People who had polio were left with fewer healthy nerves and muscles. They depended more on the healthy ones. Aging added more wear and tear.

Some polio survivors have become well-known. Henry

Dr. Albert Sabin speaks to a young family outside a polio vaccine distribution center in Cincinnati, Ohio, in 1960. Sabin invented a new form of polio vaccine in 1957.

Holden was only four years old during the 1952 epidemic. He became an actor and public speaker. He finished the Los Angeles marathon in his wheelchair. Holden is also a scuba diver, skier, and bowler. He has spent a lot of time teaching others about disabilities.[9]

Ed Roberts became a world-famous spokesperson for the disabled. He caught polio as a teenager while living near San Francisco. Roberts had dreamed of becoming a baseball player. The disease left him paralyzed. He could move only one finger. Later, he went to college. His success opened doors for other people with disabilities.

After struggling for two years in a Philadelphia hospital and then working at Warm Springs, Hugh Gallagher went to school in England. There, he graduated with honors from Oxford University. He worked as a senator's assistant in Washington, D.C. Gallagher had been the only person in a wheelchair both in college and around Congress.

Gallagher decided that his life's work would be "the search for equal access of disabled people as a civil right."[10] He worked for laws to make public buildings, monuments, parks, hospitals, and airports accessible. Gallagher also became an author and historian. His biography of Franklin D. Roosevelt is called *Splendid*

*C*hildren stricken with polio in Ethiopia, Africa, play with a ball in 1997. Polio remains a health threat in many countries outside of the United States.

Deception. He even went to Alaska and fulfilled his dream of riding a dogsled.

Many polio survivors describe what they learned from their struggles. Some say that they grew more patient and understanding. Many learned to work extra hard. They succeeded in many areas of life. Sandi Hall said, "I learned to . . . try harder, strive more, give 200% of myself and show people that just because I had polio didn't mean I [was] any less a person."[11]

Hugh Gallagher wrote, "I learned a lot about life and what's important and what isn't. . . . It was as though I'd been, say, upstairs in a house, and I knew what was upstairs. But my friends only lived on the ground floor and they didn't know there was a second floor. It was just an additional amount of knowledge. Everybody learns it, but usually it takes a lifetime. I learned it in a period of days."[12]

Other Disease Outbreaks

NAME	DATE	PLACE	DESCRIPTION
AIDS	1981–present	Worldwide	An estimated 270,000 people will die from AIDS every year.
Bubonic Plague	1347–1351	Western Europe	"The Black Death" wipes out almost half of Western Europe's population at the time.
Diphtheria	1920–1929	United States	About 150,000 cases and 13,000 deaths reported each year between 1920 and 1930.
Ebola	1976 and 1995	Zaire, Africa	318 cases, 280 deaths in 1976; 244 deaths in 1995.
Legionnaire's Disease	1976	Philadelphia	Thirty deaths.
Measles	1530–1545	Mexico	An estimated 1.5 million deaths.
Malaria	1947	India	About 1 million deaths.
Smallpox	Up to 1958	Worldwide	Killed millions of people before being virtually eliminated by vaccination.
Spanish Flu (Influenza)	1918–1919	Worldwide	20 million die as a result of the Spanish Flu.
Syphilis	1500–1550	Europe	About 10 million deaths.
Tuberculosis	1860s–present	United States	Up to 1940, had killed more people in the U.S. than any other infectious disease.
Typhus	1812	Russia	About 220,000 deaths.
West Nile Virus	1999	New York City area	Fifty cases reported, five deaths.
Yellow Fever	1960–1962	Ethiopia, Africa	An estimated 30,000 deaths.

Chapter 1. Summer Fears

1. Nina Gilden Seavey, *A Paralyzing Fear: The Story of Polio in America*, PBS Documentary, first national broadcast October 5, 1998.

2. Kacee Hargrave, "Former Doctor Chase Recalls Life During Polio Epidemic," *The San Angelo Standard-Times Online*, February 20, 1997, <http://www.texaswest.com/standard-times/news/97/feb/20/13.htm> (March 14, 2000).

3. Richard Hill, "Years of Breathless Happiness," *Museum of the Iron Lung*, n.d., <http://members.xoom.com/_XMCM/lungmuseum/responaut.htm> (March 14, 2000).

4. Nina Gilden Seavey, Jane S. Smith, and Paul Wagner, *A Paralyzing Fear: The Triumph Over Polio in America* (New York: TV Books, 1998), p. 51.

5. Ibid., p. 52.

Chapter 2. A Crippling Virus

1. John R. Paul, *A History of Poliomyelitis*, (New Haven: Yale University Press, 1971), p. 28.

2. Eleanor Wilson, writing for the *Fort-Worth Star Telegram*, quoted in Bill Fairley, "Polio Swept City, World in '40s, '50s," March 4, 1998, <http://www.virtualtexan.com/fairley/mar4.htm> (March 14, 2000).

3. Huntly Collins, "Josephine Walker: 'Lord of the Flies' in Polio Ward," *Philadelphia Enquirer*, February 23, 1999, <http://www.philly.com/packages/polio/text/surv23.asp> (March 14, 2000).

Chapter 3. Quarantine!

1. Michelle Grovak, "Early Health Care Fraught with Quackery," *Lafayette Journal and Courier*, n.d., <http://www.lafayettejc.com/special_sections/progress/stories/story14.html> (March 14, 2000).

2. Richard Carter, *Breakthrough: The Saga of Jonas Salk* (New York: Trident, 1966), p. 107.

3. Jane S. Smith, *Patenting the Sun*, (New York: Random House, 1993), p. 155.

4. Pat Zacharias, "Conquering the Dreaded Crippler, Polio," *The Detroit News*, n.d., <http://www.detroitnews.com/history/polio/polio.htm> (March 14, 2000).

5. Amy Gardner, "Glynda's Bout With Polio as a Child," *Meet Glynda Gardner, The Story of My Life*, n.d., <http://www.prys.net/forgotten/glynda.htm> (March 14, 2000).

6. Nina Gilden Seavey, Jane S. Smith, and Paul Wagner, *A Paralyzing Fear: The Triumph Over Polio in America* (New York: TV Books, 1998), pp. 77–78.

7. Ibid., p. 78.

8. Richard Hill, "Years of Breathless Happiness," *Museum of the Iron Lung*, n.d., <http://members.xoom.com/_XMCM/lungmuseum/responaut.htm> (March 14, 2000).

9. Omega Baker, "Iron Lung," *Winchester Star*, April 3, 1995, <http://www.ccms.net/~omegab/ironlung.html> (March 14, 2000).

10. Huntly Collins, "Iron Lungs and Isolation: Tales of the Polio Years," *Philadelphia Enquirer*, February 23, 1999, <http://www.philly.com/packages/polio/text/surv23.asp> (March 14, 2000).

Chapter 4. A Brave Fight

1. Edward Shorter, *The Health Century* (New York: Doubleday, 1987), p. 63.

2. Nina Gilden Seavey, Jane S. Smith, and Paul Wagner, *A Paralyzing Fear: The Triumph Over Polio in America* (New York: TV Books, 1998), p. 54.

3. Tony Gould, *A Summer Plague: Polio and Its Survivors* (New Haven: Yale University Press, 1995), p. 291.

4. Ibid., p. 290.

5. Michelle Grovak, "Early Health Care Fraught with Quackery," *Lafayette Journal and Courier*, n.d., <http://www.lafayettejc.com/special_sections/progress/stories/story14.html> (March 14, 2000).

6. Seavey, Smith, and Wagner, p. 54.

7. Jane S. Smith, *Patenting the Sun*, (New York: Random House, 1993), p. 155.

8. Richard Hill, "Years of Breathless Happiness," *Museum of the Iron Lung*, n.d., <http://members.xoom.com/_XMCM/lungmuseum/responaut.htm> (March 14, 2000).

9. Seavey, Smith, and Wagner, p. 57.

10. Margaret Stewart, "Meet Margaret Stewart," n.d., <http://www.prys.net/forgotten/mstewart.html> (March 14, 2000).

11. Sharon Karber, "Through a Child's Eyes: A Child's Polio Experience," *Immunization Action Coalition Express*, November 9, 1998, <http://www.immunize.org/genr.d/issue29.htm> (March 14, 2000).

12. Sandi Hall, "I Am a Survivor," n.d., <http://www.prys.net/forgotten/sandi.html> (March 14, 2000).

Chapter 5. "Freedom from Fear"

1. Richard Carter, *Breakthrough: The Saga of Jonas Salk* (New York: Trident, 1966), p. 107.

2. Marc Selvaggio, "The Making of Jonas Salk," *Pittsburgh*, June 1984, p. 44.

3. Jane S. Smith, *Patenting the Sun*, (New York: Random House, 1993), p. 136.

4. Ibid., p. 22.

5. Pat Zacharias, "Conquering the Dreaded Crippler, Polio," *The Detroit News*, n.d., <http://www.detroitnews.com/history/polio/polio.htm> (March 14, 2000).

6. Jim Barrett, "Polio and the Era of Fear," *The Mission*, Fall 1994, <http://www.uthscsa.edu/mission/fall94/polio.htm> (March 14, 2000).

7. Greer Williams, *Virus Hunters*, (New York: Knopf, 1959), p. 270.

8. Nadine Brozan, "Chronicle," *The New York Times*, April 13, 1999, p. D26.

9. Melissa Roof, "National Speaker Addresses Disabilities," *The University of Illinois at Springfield Journal Online*, April 14, 1999, <http://journal.uis.edu/online/4-14-99/disability.html> (March 14, 2000).

10. Hugh G. Gallagher, *Black Bird Fly Away: Disabled in An Able-Bodied World* (Arlington, Va.: Vandamere Press, 1994), p. 107.

11. Sandi Hall, "I Am a Survivor," n.d., <http://www.prys.net/forgotten/sandi.html> (March 14, 2000).

12. Nina Gilden Seavey, Jane S. Smith, and Paul Wagner, *A Paralyzing Fear: The Triumph Over Polio in America* (New York: TV Books, 1998), p. 59.

antibodies—Proteins that act in the immune system. Having antibodies for a disease helps protect a person from getting that disease.

contagious—Spreading by person-to-person contact.

epidemic—The spread of a disease to many people over a large area very quickly.

immune system—The system that protects the body from diseases and foreign substances.

immunity—Power to resist a disease.

infection—Any disease caused by germs.

iron lung—A respiration chamber that forces air into and out of a person's lungs.

motor nerves—Nerves that control muscle movements.

nerves—Tissues that carry signals between the body and the brain.

nervous system—System of nerves in the body.

outbreak—A sudden increase in occurrence.

paralysis—Loss of movement or feeling in part of the body.

poliomyelitis—An infectious viral disease that often paralyzes muscles. Known as "polio" for short.

respirator—A device that helps a person breathe.

spasm—The involuntary contraction (or twitching) of a muscle.

vaccine—A treatment that increases immunity to a disease.

virus—A tiny organism that lives inside the cells of other living things. Viruses usually spread disease.

Further Reading

Aaseng, Nathan. *Autoimmune Diseases*. Danbury, Conn.: Watts, Franklin Inc., 1995.

Bredeson, Carmen. *Jonas Salk: Discoverer of the Polio Vaccine*. Berkeley Heights, N.J.: Enslow Publishers, Inc., 1993.

Friedlander, Mark P., Jr. *Outbreak: Disease Detectives at Work*. Minneapolis, Minn.: The Lerner Publishing Group, 2000.

Kehret, Peg. *Small Steps: The Year I Got Polio*. Grove, Ill.: Whitman, Albert & Company, 1996.

Sherrow, Victoria. *Jonas Salk*. New York: Facts On File, 1993.

Spies, Karen Bornemann. *Franklin D. Roosevelt*. Berkeley Heights, N.J.: Enslow Publishers, Inc., 1999.

Internet Addresses

Discovery Channel: Epidemic!
http://www.discovery.com/exp/epidemic/epidemic.html

International Polio Victims Response Committee
http://www.congo-pages.org/ipvrc/home.htm

The March of Dimes
http://www.modimes.org

A Paralyzing Fear: The Story of Polio in America
http://www.pbs.org/storyofpolio/polio/index.html

Index